Script Your Success
Mastering the Art of Business Communication

Table of Contents

Chapter 1. Introduction

Unleash your potential and script your own success story with our Special Report: "Script Your Success: Mastering the Art of Business Communication". This exciting, straightforward, and highly actionable guide will empower you to navigate seamlessly through business environments with your words. It is more than just a report; it's your passport to triumph in the world of business. Loaded with insights, tips, and practical exercises, this report will leave you poised to engage, influence, and dazzle. Whether you are a novice entrepreneur or a seasoned business veteran, mastering business communication has never been more crucial or achievable. Crafted with cheerful enthusiasm, rich research, and objective clarity, this report will motivate and equip you to turn every business conversation into an opportunity. Purchase your copy today and step into a future where every word you utter propels you towards success.

Chapter 2. Mastering the Basics: The Key Elements of Business Communication

Business communication is a vast, intricate and dynamic field, both an art and a science. It extends far beyond the mere act of speaking or typing; it involves connecting, interacting and leaving a lasting impact. To master this complex discipline, you first need to understand its fundamental dimensions.

2.1. Understanding the Importance of Business Communication

We exist in a world thriving on communication, where enterprises are built on conversations, and leaders are molded through their words. Business communication forms the backbone of any organization's operations and plays a decisive role in its growth and sustainability.

Not only does it enable the sharing of information, ideas, and thoughts within and beyond the organization, but it also paves the way for better decision making, stronger business relationships, and a positive work environment. Your ability to communicate your thoughts efficiently and effectively could spell the difference between a missed opportunity and a profitable deal.

2.2. Setting the Communication Objectives

Before plunging headlong into business communication, it's essential to determine your communication objectives. Every message you transmit should serve a purpose, whether it's to inform, persuade, motivate, or entertain. Clear objectives provide a roadmap for your communication, directing the choice of words, tone, and platforms. They also allow you to measure the success of your communication based on the responses and feedback received.

2.3. Identifying the Audience

Arguably, your audience is the most critical factor in shaping your business communication. Understanding your audience means evaluating their knowledge, needs, expectations, and responses to your message. Are they your employees, your investors, your clients, a business partner, or the public? Each audience requires a different approach, tone, and style. In business communication, one size does not fit all.

2.4. Choosing the Right Medium

From face-to-face meetings to emails, phone calls, text messages, social media platforms, and formal business letters, the medium you choose can significantly impact your communication's effectiveness. While a face-to-face or phone conversation may be perfect for a quick, informal chat or urgent issues, emails and letters work better for formal, lengthy, or complex matters. Your choice of medium should align with the message, audience, and objectives of your communication.

2.5. Crafting the Message

Once you've conducted your preliminary analysis, it's time to craft your message, which involves deciding what to say and how to say it. Effective business communication is clear, concise, and coherent. It steers away from jargon and ambiguity. Be direct, stay focused on the topic, and most importantly, ensure your message is understood the way you intended.

2.6. Listening is as Important as Speaking

Mastering business communication is not just about delivering messages but also about attentively listening and absorbing information. When you listen, you learn, develop empathy, build mutual respect, and encourage open dialogue. Your ability to listen establishes an environment of trust, where your stakeholders feel valued and heard.

2.7. Non-Verbal Communication

Another facet of business communication often overlooked is non-verbal communication. Gestures, facial expressions, body language, and eye contact convey volumes about your state of mind and attitudes. Aligning your non-verbal signals with your words strengthens the credibility of your message.

2.8. Following Up

Communication is not a one-off process. To ensure your message has been understood and acted upon, follow-ups are essential. They also provide valuable feedback, helping you refine your future communication strategies.

Business communication is a stepping stone to business success. Your ability to transmit ideas, influence people, and build relationships hinges on your mastery of this profound skill. Master these basics, and you are well on your way to becoming an effective business communicator.

Remember, successful business communication doesn't stop at

speaking fluently or writing flawlessly; it's about creating a meaningful dialogue, creating relationships, and achieving results. As you traverse your journey, keep refining your skills, adapting to your changing environment, and evolving your strategies. This constant evolution will keep you at the top of your game, making you stand out and ensuring your success in the world of business.

Chapter 3. The Power of Active Listening in Negotiations

The efficacy of any negotiation largely hinges on the ability to listen—truly listen—to what the other party is saying. It is not an exaggeration to state that active listening stands as one of the most pivotal skills you can cultivate to optimize your business interaction potential. This skill, a staple in the toolkit of successful negotiators worldwide, illuminates key insights that can transform conversations from mundane to magical, ensuring win-win scenarios for all parties.

3.1. Understanding Active Listening

Active listening transcends the physical act of auditory receiving; it involves comprehending, retaining and engaging in dialogues with empathy and sincerity. When you listen actively, you accredit value to the speaker's perspective, demonstrating a genuine interest in their thoughts.

Active listening is not just about you—the listener—it's also about the speaker. It involves body language, feedback, paraphrasing, clarifying questions, and other nonverbal cues that signal attentiveness and the intention to understand. Thus, active listening can forge deeper bonds of mutual respect, fostering a climate suitable for efficient negotiations.

3.2. The Value of Active Listening in Negotiations

Negotiations, by nature, involve an undercurrent of tensions, as each party seeks to obtain the best possible deal. By employing active listening, you present yourself as a collaborator rather than a competitor. This significantly reduces tension, creates an atmosphere of mutual respect, and increases the prospects of achieving mutually beneficial outcomes.

Through active listening, you can decipher the underlying needs, agreements, disagreements, and interests of the other party. This valuable knowledge offers the strategic advantage of shaping your proposals and communication to address the concerns of the others more effectively.

3.3. Building Empathy Through Active Listening

One of the cornerstones of fruitful negotiation is empathy—that is, understanding the feelings and emotions of others. Active listening fosters empathy by encouraging you to understand the context and implications of the speaker's words. Nonverbal cues, tone, context, and selection of words provide a plethora of clues about the speaker's emotional state and perspective.

Empathy helps you bridge the gap between your position and that of the other party, making it easier to work towards a mutually satisfying agreement. It also predicts the possible objections and emotional barriers that could potentially derail the negotiation.

3.4. Tips and Techniques for Mastering Active Listening

Mastering active listening is a process and requires practice. Here are some practical tips and techniques to enhance this crucial skill:

1. Show genuine interest: The act of listening must be sincere. Show

interest in the speaker's opinions and engage in the conversation without judgment.

2. Be emotionally present: Ensure you're in the right frame of mind to listen. Clear your mind of distractions and focus solely on the conversation.

3. Encourage the speaker: Offer verbal affirmations like "I see," or "Go on," to encourage the speaker. Non-verbal cues, like nodding, contribute to promoting open conversation.

4. Keep interruptions to a minimum: Allow the speaker to complete their point before you formulate and express your response.

5. Summarize and Paraphrase: Repeat in your own words what the speaker has said to confirm your understanding. This reaffirms the speaker and verifies that you've correctly grasped their viewpoint.

6. Reveal understanding through responses: Respond to the speaker in a way that shows you've comprehended and considered their input.

7. Ask probing questions: Once the speaker has had their say, ask clarifying questions to deepen your understanding.

8. Ensure consistency between verbal and non-verbal signals: Make sure that your verbal affirmations align with your body language. If a conflict occurs between verbal and non-verbal communication, the speaker could perceive it as insincere.

By developing any new skill, practice is a key. Cultivating the art of active listening is a gradual process, but the effort is worth the yield. With each conversation, active listening will become more natural, enabling you to navigate the treacherous waters of negotiation with confidence and ease, reaping benefits that extend beyond the business setting and enrich personal relationships as well.

Chapter 4. Non-Verbal Cues: Reading Between the Lines

We're consistently communicating, even when we're silent. It's estimated that 70 to 93 percent of our communication is non-verbal. This enormous consideration bears subconscious influence in our conversations, often expressing more than our words do. Understanding these signals, also known as non-verbal cues, is paramount to mastering business communication.

4.1. Body Language: The Unspoken Dialogue

Body language provides an evaluative background to the spoken message. Slouching could denote disinterest or fatigue, while a straight back indicates engagement and readiness. Facial expressions, potentially the most revealing element of the body language, can betray emotions, attitudes, and reactions. Smiling suggests openness and warmth, frowning could express disappointment or disapproval, whereas an impassive face might indicate a lack of commitment or enthusiasm.

Officialese and jargon can blur conversational intention; body language cannot. An open posture—uncrossed arms and legs, aims to foster trust and facilitate openness, and encourages reciprocation. Contrariwise, a closed posture—crossed arms or slouched shoulders—reflects disinterest or defensiveness.

Understanding body language ensures living communications become dynamic transactions, rather than mere meandering exchanges.

4.2. Eye Contact: The Intangible Connection

Eye contact is a powerful form of non-verbal communication. It builds a silent connection between individuals and exudes confidence, interest, and respect. In the Western business world, maintaining eye contact signifies attentiveness and honesty.

Furthermore, the lack of eye contact might portray deceitfulness, disinterest, or nervousness. As a rule of thumb, maintain eye contact about 70% of the time when speaking and 50% of the time when listening. This balance promotes engagement without making the other person uncomfortable.

4.3. Proxemics: The Space We Share

Proxemics, or the use of space within communication interactions, reflects perceived intimacy levels and can influence the dynamics of the conversation. It includes aspects like personal distance and space, territoriality, and workplace setup.

Business conversations typically happen at 'social distance' (4 to 12 feet). However, it needs fine-tuning to individuals' comfort levels and cultural etiquette. Also, note that people lean forward when they're interested and lean back when they're relaxed or uninterested. Making larger changes in personal space may be interpreted as aggressive, so moderation is key.

4.4. Paralanguage: Listening to What Isn't Said

Beyond the words, how something is said—the tone, pitch, volume, pace, and intonation—carries massive significance. This margin between 'what' and 'how' it is communicated is Paralanguage. For instance, you might say something positive but if the tone is sarcastic, it negates the positive content and might be viewed negatively.

Tone of voice is not just about the message we're communicating, but also how we feel about it and the person we're conversing with. Cultivating conscious awareness about one's own vocal attributes and observance of others' can profoundly enhance communication effectiveness.

4.5. Dress Code: A Visual Statement

In business, you're judged by your appearance before you utter a single word. Dress code, part of non-verbal communication, is a visual statement of who you are. It can portray your level of professionalism, competence, and respect for the situation and the audience.

For instance, consider corporate attire versus casual wear. A suit typically projects seriousness, credibility and respect, whereas casual dress can imply comfort, creativity, and approachability.

Decoding the dress code within the organizational culture and depending on the audience is vital for creating the desired impact.

4.6. Kinesics: Deciphering the Body Talk

Kinesics takes a dive into subtler elements of body language, interpreting communication through gestures, body posture, stance, and facial expressions. Gestures can either complement, regulate, substitute, or contradict verbal communication. For instance, a nod might confirm agreement, while a pump of a fist can represent success.

Practicing kinesics may not only alleviate miscommunication but also help comprehend non-apparent emotions or sentiments. Mastering this decoding could provide a significant edge in negotiations or critical engagements.

4.7. Reading Between the Lines

Interpreting non-verbal cues requires emotional intelligence and conscious practice. It's about finding the harmony between verbal and non-verbal messages, consciously using signals to channel your message, and honing the skill of reading others.

Never hasten to judge based on a single non-verbal cue. Always consider the context, the verbal message accompanying the non-verbal, and any potential culture-related implications. Remember, your interpretations should be guided by thoughtful evaluation and objective clarity.

By giving non-verbal communication the attention it deserves, we'll not merely be 'talking the talk,' but we'll be 'walking the walk,' harnessing the full tapestry of human communication to script our success story in the business expanse.

In the next chapter, we shall learn about "Listening: The Silent Communicator". Until then, keep practicing reading between the lines! Remember, every conversation is an opportunity to learn and grow.

Chapter 5. Storytelling: A Strategic Tool in Business

Storytelling has always been an integral part of human culture, a form of communication that predates the written word. It has remained relevant to this day, transforming from cave drawings, folktales, and epic poems into novels, films, and marketing campaigns. Storytelling is not just about entertaining; it is about connecting, influencing, and inspiring. In the context of business, it serves as a strategic tool for making a lasting impression and fostering relationships.

5.1. The Essence of Storytelling in Business

In business, storytelling is more than a communication technique; it is the artistry of connecting on an emotional level, making your message memorable, influencing decisions, and inspiring action. A facts-and-figures report presents information but often lacks the humanizing factor that resonates with people - a gap bridged by storytelling.

5.2. How Stories Work

The human brain is hardwired to think in narratives. When information is delivered in a story format, it becomes digestible, relatable, and memorable. Narratives engage our senses, stir our emotions, and create immersive experiences that not only are enjoyable but are also encoded into our memories. Listening to a sequence of events allows us to draw our conclusions and connect with the story on a personal level - the exact engagement necessary in business communication.

5.3. The Power of Business Storytelling

From the humble 'About Us' page on a website to the grand product launch event, storytelling has the power to turn a simple message into an influential narrative. Stories make your brand more relatable, appealing, and human. They help your audience understand the values your brand embodies, the solutions you offer, and the reasons for their necessity. By telling a story, you offer customers these insights, not with a hard sell but with engaging narratives that make them a part of your journey.

5.4. Structuring Your Business Story

A compelling story features a strong structure with characters, setting, conflict, and resolution. The character is your business or product, facing a conflict (a market need or problem), and the resolution is the solution you provide. The setting elucidates where and how the situation arises. Your business story, when structured properly, presents your product or service as the hero that resolves the major conflict of the story - the market need.

5.5. Tools for Effective Storytelling

To effectively convey your message, you must master some storytelling tools - emotion, authenticity, relatability, and simplicity. Evoke emotions to connect with your audience on a profound level. Be authentic, showing the human side of your business. Craft relatable content that resonates with your audience's experiences, and keep your story simple yet powerful for better comprehension.

5.6. Storytelling Channels in Business

There are various channels to present your business story. These include your company's website, social media platforms, video productions, podcasts, and even in-person meetings and networking events. Each platform requires a different storytelling technique tailored to its format and audience.

5.7. Implementing Storytelling in Business Strategy

When implemented strategically, storytelling can attract potential customers, inspire loyalty among existing customers, and broadly increase your company's visibility and reputation. This strategy requires assessing your audience, tailoring your story per their needs and experiences, and invoking a call to action.

In conclusion, storytelling forms a central part of business communication. Being a good storyteller means being a good communicator, a compelling narrator who can lead your audience on a journey that will make your business unforgettable. By mastering this art, you can differentiate your brand, resonate with your audience, and ultimately script your success.

Chapter 6. Persuasion Techniques: Influencing with Impact

In the realm of business, persuasion is an integral skill that differentiates ordinary communicators from extraordinarily effective ones. To successfully persuade is to skillfully weave together strategic arguments and communicate them with conviction, allowing you to wield influence and create impact.

6.1. The Science Behind Persuasion

The first step to mastering the art of persuasion is to understand its foundations in psychology. Harvard psychologist, Robert Cialdini, outlined six principles of persuasion that are key tools in the arsenal of any persuasive communicator.

1. **Reciprocity**: People feel obliged to return a favor. Hence, when you give something – a concession, a gift, a favor – it prompts the receiver to feel compelled to reciprocate. In business communication, this might look like offering valuable information or assistance without expecting anything immediately in return.

2. **Commitment and Consistency**: People tend to stay consistent with their prior commitments and statements. If someone has publicly committed to something, they are more likely to follow through. Gaining smaller commitments can open the way for bigger ones.

3. **Social Proof**: People look for guidance from others and follow the crowd. Testimonials and recommendations are powerful tools in persuasion as they provide this social proof.

4. **Authority**: People tend to obey people in positions of authority or those who demonstrate expertise. Establishing yourself as an authority in your field makes your arguments more persuasive.

5. **Liking**: People are more likely to be persuaded by someone they like. Build rapport and show empathy to increase your likability.

6. **Scarcity**: Items or opportunities are more attractive if they are limited. Creating a sense of urgency or exclusivity can make your proposal more persuasive.

Developing a deep understanding of these principles is a foundational step towards becoming a persuasive communicator.

6.2. Building a Persuasive Argument

A persuasive argument is not constructed haphazardly but is thoughtfully planned and executed. To craft a compelling argument, it's necessary to understand the audience's needs, establish credibility, provide strong evidence, and call to action.

1. **Understand Your Audience**: To persuade effectively, you must first understand your audience and their needs. This involves identifying their perspective, interests, desires, and potential barriers. Tailoring your message to appeal to these needs will make your arguments more compelling.

2. **Establish Credibility**: Trust is a vital factor in persuasion. It's critical to establish your credibility early. Credibility can be built by demonstrating expertise, sincerity, and reliability.

3. **Provide Strong Evidence**: Evidence strengthens your argument and adds validity. The more relevant and strong your evidence, the more persuasive your argument becomes. Evidence can include statistical data, facts, quotes, examples, or results from studies and research.

4. **Call to Action**: End your argument with a strong and direct call-

to-action. Make it clear what action you want your audience to take and why it's beneficial to them.

Remember, persuasive communication is not about manipulation, but about convincing others through ethically sound arguments.

6.3. The Power of Narrative in Persuasion

Stories possess a unique power to persuade by engaging listeners on an emotional level. When crafting stories for persuasion, consider the following elements:

1. **Character**: Characters form the heart of any narrative. In business communication, the primary character should be the audience or a character they can empathize with.

2. **Plot**: The plot should present a problem or challenge faced by the character, and how it is resolved. This plot should align with the message you want to convey.

3. **Message**: The message is the idea you want to impart. It should be woven subtly throughout the plot and made explicit in the end.

Crafting compelling stories can turn complex ideas into accessible concepts and engage your audience at a deeper level.

6.4. The Art of Rhetoric: Ethos, Pathos, and Logos

Greek philosopher Aristotle identified three modes of persuasion that remain relevant today: Ethos (Ethical Appeal), Pathos (Emotional Appeal), and Logos (Logical Appeal).

- Ethos: Relying on the speaker's credibility or character. Establish your expertise and trustworthiness to ensure your audience believes in you and your message.

- Pathos: Playing on emotions can effectively persuade the audience. Use stories, strong imagery, or emotive language to elicit feelings.

- Logos: Using logical arguments and sound reasoning. Provide sound evidence and logical reasoning to back your claims.

It's beneficial to balance all the three modes of persuasion in business communication. The right balance can make the difference between a persuasive argument and one that falls flat.

6.5. Non-Verbal Persuasion Techniques

When it comes to persuasion, non-verbal communication plays a significant role. Elements such as body language, tone of voice, facial expressions, and eye contact can either strengthen or weaken your message.

1. **Body language**: Positive body language, like upright posture and open gestures, can signal confidence and credibility. Conversely, defensive or closed body language can undermine your message.

2. **Tone of voice**: A confident and engaging tone can draw listeners in and command their attention. Varying your pitch, volume, and speed can also add emphasis and help convey your message effectively.

3. **Facial Expressions**: Your facial expressions can communicate emotions and attitudes, adding depth and sincerity to your message.

4. **Eye Contact**: Maintaining eye contact can convey confidence and establish a connection with your audience, increasing your

persuasive power.

Understanding and leveraging non-verbal communication techniques can significantly enhance your ability to persuade.

With these techniques and strategies at your disposal, you are well-equipped to begin your journey toward becoming a true master of persuasive business communication.

Chapter 7. Emotional Intelligence in Work Conversations

Emotional intelligence, or EQ, is the ability to understand, use, and manage our own emotions in positive ways to relieve stress, communicate effectively, empathize with others, overcome challenges and defuse conflict. It's the comprehensive set of skills that all of us use in every part of our lives which shape our behavior and navigate our social complexities. In the context of work conversations, emotional intelligence plays a paramount role in achieving a productive conversation and establishing robust relationships.

7.1. Importance of Emotional Intelligence

Emotional intelligence lays at the heart of the most human of interactions which include work conversations. It influences our capacity to communicate effectively and maintain relationships professionally. Developing and honing emotional intelligence can not just strengthen existing interpersonal connections, but can also open doors to new ones by enhancing self-awareness and offering a well-rounded perspective in varying situations.

1. **Leadership**: For those in leadership positions, EQ is critical in shaping a productive and harmonious team. Leaders with high emotional intelligence exhibit empathy towards their team members, understand their feelings, and respond accordingly. This assists in maintaining team harmony and increasing overall productivity.

2. **Conflict Resolution**: Emotional intelligence equips individuals with the proficiency to manage and resolve conflicts efficiently, avoiding unnecessary escalation.

3. **Decision Making**: Emotional intelligence permits a solid balance between rational considerations and emotional aspects while making decisions, which leads to better-quality and well-thought-out outcomes.

7.2. Recognizing Emotion

One of the starting points of developing emotional intelligence is in recognizing emotion – both in yourself and others. Recognizing an emotion translates to understanding how you're feeling, or how someone else might be feeling based on verbal and non-verbal cues.

1. **Recognizing Your Own Emotion**: It's crucial to tune into your emotional state. As emotions are transient, they constantly change according to various influences. Cultivating a habit of self-reflection and -assessment can help you recognize and label your emotions better. Spend a few moments each day to introspect and identify what you're feeling. By doing so, you'll be better equipped to manage your emotions during work conversations.

2. **Recognizing Emotions In Others**: Every person conveys emotions differently - some are vocal while others may rely on non-verbal cues like body language, eye contact, and facial expressions. It's essential to be observant of these cues during conversations. As you become more attuned to these signals, you will find it easier to perceive the emotions of others, enabling more effective communication.

7.3. Managing Emotions

Upon recognizing your emotions, the next step is learning to manage them. This does not imply suppressing or ignoring them. Instead, managing emotions involves understanding them, acknowledging their presence, and ensuring they do not dictate your reaction or decisions.

1. **Timeout**: If an emotion is overwhelming, it's okay to pause and process it before responding to a situation. A few deep breaths or a short break can provide space to realign thoughts.

2. **Constructive Channeling**: Positive and negative emotions significantly influence creativity. Use this to your advantage by channeling them constructively. For instance, anxiety could be channeled into preparation or review, while excitement could be directed towards productive brainstorming.

3. **Respond, Don't React**: In emotionally charged situations, it's crucial to make a conscious decision to respond rather than react. Responding allows you to consider various factors and potential consequences, while reacting is often immediate and without thought of the repercussions.

7.4. Enhancing Emotional Intelligence

While inherent to a degree, emotional intelligence can certainly be enhanced with consistent effort and awareness. Here are a few suggestions:

1. **Practice Active Listening**: Actively listen during conversations instead of merely waiting for your turn to talk. This allows you to understand the other person's viewpoint and respond thoughtfully.

2. **Improve Self-awareness**: Cultivate the habit of regular introspection to understand how you're feeling and why. Identify triggers and patterns in your emotional responses.

3. **Develop Empathy**: Try to put yourself in another person's shoes and see the situation from their perspective. This can significantly improve your understanding of others' emotions.

Developing and utilizing emotional intelligence can make your work conversations more effective, meaningful and productive. As emotional intelligence is intrinsic to all interpersonal interactions, nourishing this skill significantly enhances overall communication skills. Remember, emotional intelligence is a continuous learning journey, echoing in the words of renowned psychologist Daniel Goleman, "Emotional intelligence is not fixed. It is a flexible skill that can be improved with increased awareness, practice, and a commitment to personal growth."

Chapter 8. Conflict Resolution: Effective Strategies for Disagreeing Diplomatically

Effective communication involves more than simply expressing ideas or sharing information. It is about understanding the emotions and intentions behind the information. This is especially true when disagreements arise in business scenarios. It gives companies the opportunity to thrive by fostering better relationships among team members and partners alike. The following approach will provide you with the tools you need to agree to disagree with dignity and carry forward the spirit of positive discourse.

8.1. The Science of Disagreement

Disagreements are a natural part of human interaction. They are not inherently negative. They often spark creativity and can propel teams towards finding innovative solutions to complex problems. Understanding this concept is the first step towards embracing healthy conflict.

People have different viewpoints due to their varied experiences, personalities, and perspectives. Divergent thinking can help to constructively use these differences to achieve common goals. Recognizing the benefits of conflict can transform it from a dreaded confrontation into an opportunity for growth and learning.

8.2. Active Listening: The Power of Understanding

Active listening is a cornerstone of effective communication and conflict resolution. It requires more than just hearing the speaker's words. It mandates understanding the message, interpreting the emotions behind it, and responding thoughtfully. Active listening demonstrates respect for the speaker's viewpoint and fosters open and meaningful discourse.

Here are some key steps to embrace active listening:

1. Encourage open dialog: Encourage the speaker to express themselves freely without interruption.

2. Focus on the speaker: Facilitate a distraction-free environment to show that the speaker's thoughts and feelings are being valued.

3. Paraphrase and clarify: Repeat their point in your own words to confirm understanding. Ask clarifying questions if unsure.

4. Provide feedback: Use non-verbal clues like nodding or brief verbal confirmations like "I see" or "go on" to indicate you are fully engaged.

Practicing active listening assures the opponent that their thoughts and feelings are being acknowledged, which can help diffuse any negative emotions.

8.3. Emotional Intelligence: The Secret Weapon

Emotional Intelligence (EI) in a conflict situation is akin to bringing a secret weapon to the battlefield. EI is the ability to identify, use, understand, and manage emotions in an effective and positive way. High levels of EI lead to improved problem-solving capacity, better conflict resolution skills, and enhanced communication.

Practicing emotional intelligence in conflict resolution involves:

1. Self-awareness: Being aware of your emotions, triggers and reactions.
2. Self-management: Controlling impulsive feelings and behaviors, managing your emotions in healthy ways.
3. Empathy: Understanding, and sharing the feelings of others.
4. Relationship management: Establishing good relations with others, managing conflicts constructively.

By boosting your EI, you can maintain your composure during disagreements, understand core issues, and foster a positive environment for conflict resolution.

8.4. Assertiveness vs Aggressiveness

There's a fine line between assertiveness and aggressiveness. While the former is crucial for effective conflict resolution, the latter can inhibit the process. Assertiveness involves expressing your thoughts and feelings in a respectful and honest manner, whereas aggressiveness includes imposing one's views on others disrespectfully.

The key to staying assertive, not aggressive during conflicts involves:

1. Stating your needs clearly: Be clear and honest about what you want, need, or feel.
2. Using "I" statements: This personalizes your thoughts and feelings, and prevents blaming the other person.
3. Striving for mutual understanding: Show willingness for finding a common ground.
4. Listening and acknowledging: Give others a fair chance to

express their thoughts and feelings.

By focusing on assertive communication, you can ensure that all viewpoints are respected and considered.

8.5. Structured Problem-Solving

In any conflict situation, the primary aim should be to solve the problem, not to win the argument. The use of structured problem-solving techniques can be highly beneficial in achieving this goal. It can ensure that all involved parties agree to desirable solutions.

Follow the steps below:

1. Identify and understand the issue: Define the problem in specific terms.

2. Communicate openly: Encourage all parties to express their feelings and thoughts related to the problem.

3. Develop possible solutions: Brainstorm solutions, encouraging all parties to participate.

4. Evaluate each solution: Discuss pros and cons of each option objectively.

5. Decide on a solution: cooperatively choose the best solution. This mutual agreement can facilitate successful resolution.

6. Implement the solution: Create a plan to execute the solution and assign responsibilities.

7. Follow-up: Assess and discuss whether the solution has effectively resolved the issue or not.

This approach helps to diffuse negative emotions, foster collective decision-making, and promote responsibility and ownership of the solution.

Negotiation, compromise, and conflict resolution are crucial skills in the business world. Mastering them doesn't mean eradicating all conflicts. Rather, it means leveraging conflicts as opportunities for growth, learning, and innovation. With the skills and strategies outlined in this chapter, you're now equipped to disagree diplomatically and lead teams towards harmonious business solutions.

Chapter 9. Cross-Cultural Communication: Bridging Diverse Business Environments

The world of business is indeed a global village. It's a colossal network interconnecting different cultures, traditions, and ways of communication. As a business professional, engaging in cross-cultural communication is often inevitable and mastering it crucial.

9.1. The Essence of Cross-Cultural Communication

Cross-cultural communication refers to the process of sharing, negotiating, and mediating one's cultural differences through language, non-verbal gestures, and space relationships. It plays an integral role in the business environment by allowing dissimilar cultures to learn from each other, promote mutual understanding, and ensure effective collaboration.

In a business context, poor cross-cultural communication can lead to misunderstandings and conflicts, impacting the success of global business operations and collaborations. Understanding cultural differences, therefore, forms a foundational step in crafting effectual communication techniques across disparate cultural environments.

9.2. Navigating Cultural Communication Differences

Every culture has specific, ingrained nuances, affecting how people communicate within that culture. For instance, while direct communication, punctuality, and personal space are valued in Western cultures, high context cultures in Asia or the Middle East often prioritize indirect communication, hierarchical relationships, and collective harmony. Successful communicators are those who can navigate these differences seamlessly.

It's worth noting that non-verbal cues—facial expressions, body language, and even silence—itself can communicate certain feelings or responses in a specific culture. Witnessing and respecting these cues aids in better understanding and contributing to a culturally rich dialogue.

9.3. Understanding Cultural Dimensions

The renowned cultural model by Geert Hofstede, a Dutch social psychologist, employs six dimensions to help understand cultural differences. He coined the terms Power Distance (PDI), Individualism vs. Collectivism (IDV), Masculinity vs. Femininity (MAS), Uncertainty Avoidance (UA), Long-Term Orientation vs. Short-Term Normative Orientation (LTO), and Indulgence vs. Restraint (IND).

Exploring each of these dimensions can offer insights into potential barriers to effective communication and ways to overcome them. For instance, in high power distance cultures, decisions are often centralized, and it's important to respect hierarchical structures. Whereas, in low power distance cultures, decisions are commonly decentralized, and input is expected from everyone involved.

9.4. Mitigating Language Barriers

Language undoubtedly plays an essential role in communication. With globalization, the likelihood of operating in a non-native language for many employees has significantly increased. Hence, ensuring clarity of communication and leveraging common languages or translations becomes worthwhile.

Deployment of 'simpler' English, avoiding jargon, and adopting slower speech can aid comprehension. Additionally, it's prudent to appreciate linguistic skills, and never underestimate one's intelligence based on their English proficiency.

9.5. Cultivating Cross-Cultural Empathy

Empathy plays a pivotal role in cross-cultural communication. It enables one to understand others' perspectives and respond in a way that recognizes their feelings and culture. It puts ourselves in others' shoes, promoting more genuine, respectful conversations, which are vital to business success.

The significant aspects of developing cross-cultural empathy include cultural self-awareness, openness towards cultural learning, and respectful curiosity about different cultures. Proactive efforts towards understanding cultural differences—through books, films or take advantage of training opportunities—can help in promoting empathy and understanding in a multicultural business world.

9.6. Adapt and Embrace

No matter how much theoretical knowledge one gains about different cultures, nothing truly replaces firsthand experience. Engaging directly with people from different cultures, being open to feedback, and ready to adapt to unexpected situations ensures a more practical application of cross-cultural communication skills.

Remember, the goal of understanding cross-cultural communication isn't to stereotype or generalize, but to appreciate diversity and navigate different cultural terrains with finesse. It promotes an inclusive work environment and offers a competitive edge in the global business landscape.

In conclusion, cross-cultural communication presents both challenges and opportunities. With a mix of proactive learning, empathy, and experience, business professionals can connect on a profound level with various cultures, catalyzing effective communication, and fostering fruitful collaborations. Therefore, mastering cross-cultural communication is not just a luxury but a necessity for thriving in the diverse world of business.

This chapter hopefully provides you a roadmap to developing valuable techniques in cross-cultural communication that will propel you towards success in any business environment you step into.

Chapter 10. Email Etiquette: Right Message at the Right Time

In the digital age we're living in, email has emerged as a critical component of business communication. Ensuring proper email communication reflects your professionalism, demonstrates respect for the recipient's time, and bolsters your personal brand. Well-written emails also contribute to effective communication, reducing the risk of misinterpretation or confusion.

10.1. Understanding Email Etiquette

Think of email as you would any other form of communication. Just as there are social norms for interacting in person or on the phone, there are norms for email communication. This includes using a professional tone, remembering to include an appropriate greeting and closing, and taking time to proofread before sending.

One aspect of email etiquette that often gets overlooked is the importance of timeliness. Responding to emails in a timely manner is a must. Leaving an email unanswered for several days or even a week can make you appear unresponsive or uninterested. On the other hand, responding too quickly can make you appear too eager or desperate. A good rule of thumb is to respond within 24 hours whenever possible.

10.2. Keep it Professional

The email itself should be written in a professional manner, which means steering clear of abbreviations or slang that you might use in a text message or social media post. The subject line should clearly state the purpose of the email, and the message should get directly to the point.

Any attachments should be named appropriately, and if there are multiple attachments, consider compressing them into a single zip file for convenience.

Your signature is a vital component of your professional emails. Ensure it contains your full name and professional title, contact details, and perhaps a link to your LinkedIn profile or business website. If you have any disclaimers related to your business, ensure they are included too.

Never forget to double-check the recipients' email addresses to ensure they are correct before hitting the send button. A simple slip can make your email land in a wrong inbox, a mistake which could be fatal depending on the sensitivity of the information.

10.3. Writing Clearly and Precisely

Clear and precise writing means your readers do not have to work hard to understand your message. Properly structure your content, using paragraphs to separate different ideas, bullets to list items and bold or italics to emphasize important points.

Even though you want to write professionally, it doesn't mean your emails should be filled with jargon. Unless you're correspondencing with someone in your field who you know will understand it, replace technical terms with simpler language.

When giving feedback or discussing sensitive topics, try to use the sandwich approach — start and end with positive comments, and put the criticism or difficult issues in the middle. This helps to soften the blow and makes it more likely the recipient will be receptive to your message.

10.4. The Art of Follow-Ups

There's an art to sending effective follow-up emails without seeming bothersome. Start the email by gently reminding the recipient of the initial email, and then state why you're following up. Is there information you're waiting on? Was there a question you asked that hasn't been answered? Is there a deadline approaching?

While maintaining professionalism, your follow-up emails could also include some warmth, understanding that people are busy and might miss responding to some communications.

In your final paragraph, ensure to show appreciation for their time and then sign off, looking forward to their kind response.

10.5. Wrapping Up

In essence, mastering the art of business emails requires an understanding that respect, clear communication, and timeliness form the basis for successful correspondence. Email is an essential tool in your business communication arsenal, and mastering its usage not only contributes to professional success but also to the efficient running of your organization.

By applying the tips and guidelines as presented above, you're one step closer in mastering the art of business communications, and in essence, further scripting your success story in becoming a better entrepreneur or business leader.

Remember, your email communications can create lasting impressions, so always put your best foot forward, one email at a time.

Chapter 11. Digital Communication and Social Media: The New Business Norm

Digital communication and social media are no longer optional extras in the business world; they are the new norm. The rise of the internet and the ubiquity of smartphones mean that consumers are always online, always connected, and always engaging with brands digitally. As a result, businesses need to understand and master only does this trend drive business communication in the 21st century.

11.1. Understanding Digital Communication

Digital communication encompasses a broad swath of technologies, platforms, and strategies used to send and receive messages virtually. The core purpose remains the same as with traditional forms of communication – disseminating information, engaging with stakeholders, and building relationships – but the medium and methodology have changed.

With digital communication, businesses can instantly reach a wide audience, facilitate engagement in real-time, and harness the power of data for more personalized and strategic messaging. An email can be sent to thousands of customers simultaneously with a simple click. Tweets can spark conversations with consumers halfway across the globe. Data from a single digital interaction can provide actionable insights to enhance future messaging.

But while digital communication opens myriad opportunities, it also poses challenges. Businesses must navigate issues like information overload, digital security, and the delicate balance of personalization versus privacy. Overcoming these challenges requires understanding each platform's unique characteristics, the intended audience and their behavior, and the intricacies of crafting a compelling digital message.

11.2. The Power of Social Media

Social media is an integral part of the digital communication landscape. Platforms like Facebook, Twitter, Instagram, and LinkedIn offer businesses unprecedented opportunities to connect with their customers on a personal basis. Whether it's through community-building initiatives, viral marketing campaigns, or simply responding to customer queries in the comments, social media platforms facilitate meaningful dialogue between brands and consumers.

Moreover, the capacity for user-generated content — comments, reviews, and shares — has democratized the marketing process. Brands are no longer the sole producers of their narrative. Consumers contribute to the brand story through their engagement, and their shared experiences can influence public perception.

However, to optimize social media usage, businesses must strategize beyond merely setting up profiles and posting regularly. They need to consistently produce high-quality, relevant content that resonates with their audience; cultivate a unique brand voice; and analyze data to measure their efforts' effectiveness.

11.3. Strategies for Effective Digital Communication

Effective digital communication hinges on several key principles: clear and concise messaging, empathy, personalization, responsiveness, and consistency.

Clear and concise messaging is particularly crucial in a landscape where consumers are bombarded with content. Your message must quickly capture attention and be easy to understand.

Empathy, understanding your audience's needs and concerns, leads to more significant engagement. By speaking to their emotions, aspirations, or pain points, you are likely to spark interest and elicit action.

Personalization involves tailoring your message to the receiver, which makes them feel valued and understood. Email marketing, for example, allows for deep customization - from addressing the recipient by name to modifying content based on their preferences.

Responsiveness reflects your commitment to customer satisfaction, and it's especially important online where communication is real-time.

Consistency in messaging across different online platforms strengthens your brand's identity and credibility. It guides what consumers can expect when interacting with your brand.

11.4. Managing Digital Communication Challenges

While digital communication offers many opportunities, managing its challenges is equally crucial. These challenges can range from security concerns to maintaining privacy and addressing the issue of misinformation.

A robust security protocol is essential to protect your organization's and customers' sensitive data. It's imperative to keep software solutions updated, use reliable security tools and train employees to recognize potential threats.

Privacy concerns have risen alongside increased digital communication. Respect your target audience's privacy by being transparent about how their data will be used and giving them options to customize their interaction with your digital communication channels.

As for misinformation, online information is susceptible to manipulation and spreading unchecked. This can harm a company's reputation and relationship with its customers. By verifying all shared information, correcting mistakes promptly, and being transparent, businesses can mitigate misinformation's impact.

11.5. Measuring Digital Communication Success

Finally, businesses need to measure digital communication success to understand the effectiveness of their strategies and find ways to improve. Key performance indicators can include metrics like click-through rates, conversions, comments, shares, likes, and other forms of engagement.

Tools like Google Analytics, Facebook Insights, and various social listening tools can lend invaluable insights into your digital communication strategy's effectiveness.

In the end, digital communication and social media have transformed the way businesses interact with their customers. By understanding the landscape, developing effective strategies, managing challenges, and measuring success, businesses can leverage these powerful tools to enhance their brand, engage with their customers, and ultimately drive success in the digital age.